P9-DMC-527

GO tennis

Rolf Flichtbeil

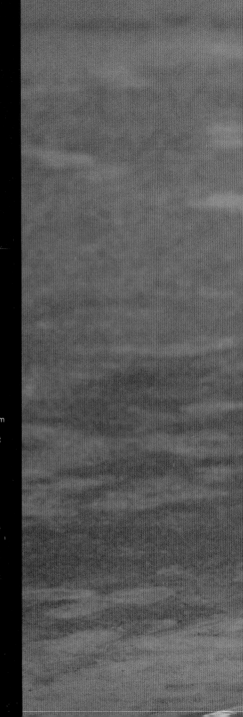

London, New York, Munich, Melbourne, Delhi

Project Editor **Nicky Munro**
Project Art Editor **Jenisa Patel**
DTP Designer **Vania Cunha**
Production Controller **Melanie Dowland**
Managing Editor **Stephanie Farrow**
Managing Art Editor **Lee Griffiths**
Photography **Gerard Brown**

Produced for Dorling Kindersley by
XAB Design, London
Design **Beverley Speight, Nigel Wright**
Editorial **Liz Dean**

DVD produced for Dorling Kindersley by
Chrome Productions www.chromeproductions.com
Director **Gez Medinger**
Camera **Neil Gordon**
Production Manager **Portia Mishcon**
Production Assistant **Jolyon Rubinstein**
Voiceover **Kevin Harris**
Voiceover Recording **Mark Maclaine**
Music **Scott Shields**, produced by **FMPTV**

First American Edition, 2006

First published in the United States by
DK Publishing, Inc., 375 Hudson Street,
New York, NY 10014

06 07 08 09 10 10 9 8 7 6 5 4 3 2 1

Copyright © 2006 Dorling Kindersley Limited

A Cataloging-in-Publication record for this book is available from
the Library of Congress.

ISBN-13: 978-0-7566-1942-8
ISBN-10: 0-7566-1942-4

DK books are available at special discounts for bulk purchases for
sales promotions, premiums, fund-raising, or educational use.
For details, contact: DK Publishing Special Markets, 375 Hudson
Street, New York, NY 10014 or SpecialSales@dk.com

Color reproduction by Icon Reproduction, UK
Printed and bound in China by Hung Hing

Discover more at

www.dk.com

contents

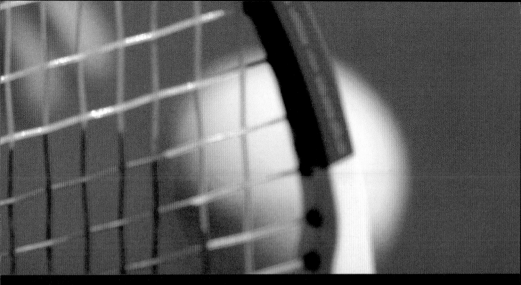

how to use this book and DVD

This fully integrated book and accompanying DVD are designed to inspire you to get out onto the court. Watch all the essential techniques on the DVD in crystal-clear, real-time footage, with key elements broken down in state-of-the-art digital graphics, and then read all about them, and more, in the book.

Using the book
Venturing onto the tennis court for the first time can seem a little nerve-wracking, so this book explains everything you need to know to start playing tennis with confidence. Cross-references to the DVD are included on pages that are backed up by footage.

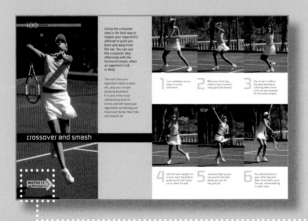

Switch on the DVD
When you see this logo in the book, check out the action in the relevant chapter of the DVD.

Using the DVD

Supporting the book with movie sequences and computer graphics, this DVD is the perfect way to see key techniques demonstrated in precise detail. Navigate to each subject using the main menu, and view sequences as often as you like to see how it's done!

Flick to the book
When you see this logo on the DVD, flick to the relevant page of the book to read all about it.

why play tennis?

Tennis is a game that has it all. It's a lot of fun, it allows you to build up both your physical and mental skills, it is hugely sociable, and it gives you the chance to enjoy the thrill of competition. Getting started is easy—all you need is a racquet, a pair of shoes, and a can of balls. Don't worry about your standard of play to begin with, just go and find a court and get involved.

This book will show you all you need to know to get started in tennis, from choosing a racquet to understanding the court and the rules of play. It shows you how to have fun learning the basics before developing your skills and adding more difficult shots, moves, and strategies to your repertoire. Before you know it, you'll be really putting the pressure on your opponents. You may even find yourself training for a tournament! Whatever level you are at, when the tennis bug bites, you can be sure of some good times ahead.

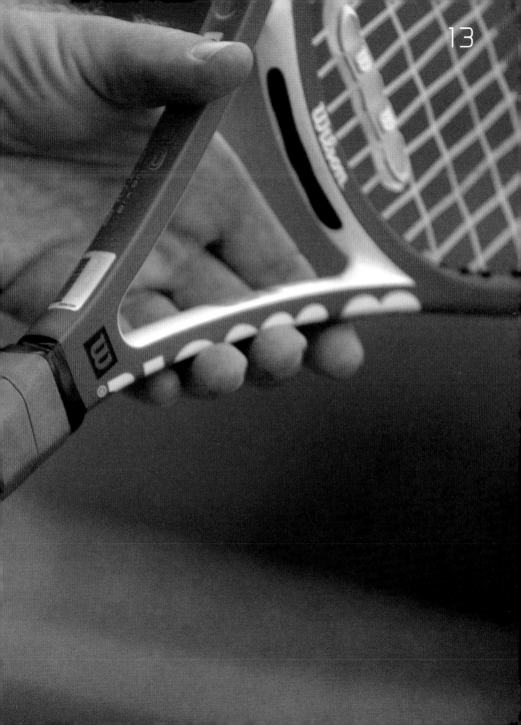

go get ready

coming up...

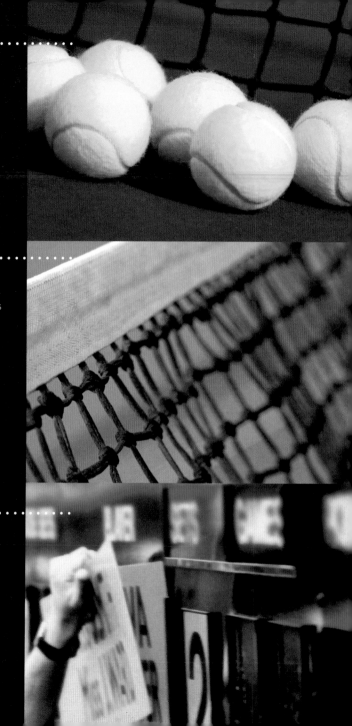

Equipment: 18–27

New technology has led to major advances in tennis equipment. Stronger, lighter materials have vastly improved racquet performance, while today's strings, balls, and clothing are designed to make the whole tennis experience more exciting and enjoyable.

Field of play: 28–31

Learn the layout and markings of the court and understand the difference between the singles and the doubles court. The net is more than just a divider strung across the middle of the court; your task is to find the best way of getting the ball over the net to win the point. Find out how different court surfaces affect play and ball speed.

Scoring and basic rules: 32–35

Before you begin, you'll need to become familiar with the scoring system and rules for singles and doubles matches. Here's a rundown of the basic rules and finer points that make the game all the more dynamic and compelling.

racquet anatomy

The tennis racquet you choose must feel good and suit your style of play, giving you the optimum balance between power and control. With today's technology and new stronger, lighter materials, manufacturers are developing top quality racquets with varying sized heads and weights that will suit all different types of player and their games.

Finding the right grip
The bevels of the racquet handle help players to relate to the position of the racquet face and find the correct grip. If you are looking at the racquet side on, the first bevel is the one that corresponds to the edge of the frame. The third bevel corresponds to the racquet face and so on (left to right for a right hander and the other way for a left hander).

Grommets
A plastic strip with grommets is placed around the racquet head to prevent racquet stress when the strings are pulled tight.

Head guard
A strip of plastic placed on the top edge of the racquet protects it from excessive wear and tear from direct contact with the court.

Frame
The frame of the racquet usually refers to the outside edge of the head. These come in various sizes and thicknesses according to the specific needs of players.

Throat
The throat of the racquet is the area between the handle and the head. This area is an open v-shape, which gives the racquet stability and cuts air resistance.

Strings
A quality set of strings can significantly enhance the performance of a racquet, and therefore your game. Simple nylon strings offer poor feel and do not last long. Gut strings offer superior feel with good durability. Most synthetic gut strings will offer a combination of good control and longevity at a reasonable price.

Handle
Handles come in various sizes to fit an individual's hand. The outer coverings are either of leather or a soft cushion grip.

Bevel
The racquet handle has eight sides that help you to find the correct grip and ensure that you have a secure hold of the handle. The flat sides of the handle are called bevels.

Butt of the handle
The butt is a plastic cover placed on the end of the handle that expands outward to form a ridge, creating a better grip. The company logo is on the base of the butt.

choosing a racquet

With practice, your tennis will rapidly improve, so buy a good-quality racquet that will work for you long-term. There are a bewildering number of different types of racquet available, with a wide range of prices. You should be looking for a racquet that improves your game and makes it more fun to play.

- Racquet heads come in various sizes. If you are a hard hitter, choose a mid-sized racquet. For extra power, choose an oversized racquet. These have a larger sweet spot (the area of maximum spring when the ball contacts the strings) and supply power even on off-center shots.

- Check your grip size by holding the handle. The grip is correct if there's a finger-width gap between your fingertips and your palm.

- An extra-long racquet gives additional reach and power. Players using a one-handed backhand should choose a standard length.

- Racquets are available in a range of weights. It is usually best to go for a mid-weight—too heavy and the racquet will be hard to maneuver, too light and it will be unstable.

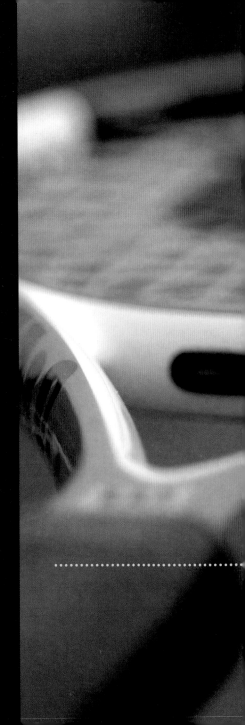

Grip
The correct grip size feels naturally comfortable.

Length
Most racquets are standard length: 27 in (67.5 cm); some are extra long— 29 in (72.5 cm).

Head size and frame thickness
If you are physically strong, buy a stiff racquet with a thin frame and a small head size.

ball facts

All major tennis-ball manufacturers make balls that conform to international regulations. Tennis balls are made of rubber and covered in a mixture of synthetic and wool fibers. They are made in two halves and the seams are covered with elastic sealant. This is the familiar wiggly line visible on the balls. Most players use pressurized balls, which come in special sealed tubes. Pressurized balls lose pressure and bounce after a while and become "dead balls." You can tell that a ball is dead if it can be squeezed easily. Unused tennis balls go through the air faster and come off court quicker, so players should hold them up before serving to indicate that they are new.

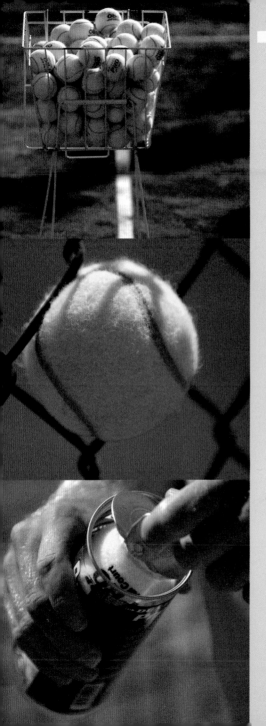

All about balls

The official color used for tennis balls is yellow or white. Yellow is the most often used as this color stands out, making it easy to follow the ball against the colors of the court or a blue sky.

A tennis ball must be between $2^1/_2$–$2^5/_8$ in (6.25–6.5 cm) in diameter and weigh between 2 oz–$2^1/_{16}$ oz (56.6–58.3 g) to be acceptable for tournament play.

• Overused balls lose their covering or go flat, which is bad for control and can place undue stress on your wrist and arm, so it is important to buy new balls regularly.

• If the fibers have become worn and fluffed up, it will slow the ball down. When players inspect a ball prior to serving, they are looking to see if it shows any signs of wear and tear.

• Pressure-less balls last for several months and maintain a uniform bounce, but bear in mind that they are less responsive and place more stress on the arm than regular pressurized balls.

• Tennis balls have to undergo rigorous testing procedures before they are approved for tournament play. However, if you are practicing with your partner or using a ball machine, second-grade balls are perfectly acceptable.

Correct tennis attire and tennis accessories are designed specifically for the rigors of the sport, and to ensure safety and comfort. In the past, there were very strict rules regarding what you were allowed to wear on the tennis court and most players wore white—in fact, many clubs required it.

Fashions in tennis clothing have changed, however, and these days, many styles and colors are acceptable that weren't tolerated even five years ago. Some well-known tennis players design their own tennis gear and these styles often filter down to major sports shops. Dress regulations for non-competitive tennis are generally free from restrictions in an effort to maximize participation at this level. To avoid embarrassment or confusion, though, it's a good idea to check whether there's a dress code at the club where you are playing.

get the gear

- Choose loose-fitting clothes for ease of movement and remember that pocket for the extra ball.

- Always wear a hat in the sun, and sunglasses if you need them.

- Cotton wrist bands absorb sweat, keeping the handle of your racquet dry and your grip firm.

Head gear
A peaked baseball hat will keep your head cool and the sun out of your eyes. White is a good choice in warm climates as it reflects the heat.

Fabric choice
Choose breathable fabrics designed for tennis to keep you cool and comfortable.

Racquet grip
A disposable overgrip absorbs sweat and prevents slippage. Because it's thinner than the grip it is placed over, the grip size is not discernably altered.

Toes

Tennis shoes are reinforced at the toes to prevent rapid wear and tear.

Uppers

Shoes have leather or mesh uppers so feet can breathe.

Padding

Padding on the shoe upper and tongue supports the foot and protects against chafing.

tennis shoes

It is important to wear shoes made specifically for tennis, because they are designed for the stop-and-start lateral movement of the sport. Your shoes need to be matched to the anatomy of your feet and the type of surface you will be playing on in order to achieve efficient and injury-free movement on the court.

Arch support
Reinforced arches support the feet and ankles, which combats arch fatigue and helps during forward sprints.

Heel support
Extra cushioning at the heel protects feet from the pounding they receive during a game.

Side reinforcement
Reinforced sides help to keep shoes in shape when you slide to reach shots on clay courts.

Different soles

- Non-marking soles should be worn for hard courts. An indoor shoe, which has a smoother, flat sole, is designed for surfaces such as carpet and wood.

- For play on a grass court, wear tennis shoes with tiny plastic studs on the sole, for grip.

- Tennis shoes with a herringbone sole are specially designed for best traction on clay courts.

Avoiding injury

- Make sure that the shoes you buy are not too tight, and wear thick cotton socks to absorb sweat and prevent blisters.

- Don't wear running shoes or training shoes as these, unlike tennis shoes, are not designed with a durable toe cap and sole to protect your feet from the rigors of the game.

zones of the court

WATCH IT
see DVD chapter 1

All tennis courts have a standard layout and measurements, and most are marked for both singles and doubles play.

A regulation tennis court is 78 ft (23.77 m) long, 27 ft (8.23 m) wide for singles play, and 36 ft (10.97 m) wide for doubles.

All courts are fenced off to stop balls from straying. The playing area is marked with white lines, which indicate if the ball is in or out. The "open court" is the opposite side from where your opponent is, assuming they are not in the middle.

The right-hand side of the court from the center mark is called the "deuce" court, and the left-hand side is called the "advantage," or "ad" court. Players change ends at the end of the first, third, fifth game and so on until the end of a set.

A net divides the court into two equal ends, and is held up by net posts at both sides. The net height at its center should be 36$^{1}/_{2}$ in (91.5 cm). Check this before the start of each match.

Doubles court sideline

Singles court sideline

Service box

Center mark

Service box

Baseline

Doubles alley or tramline area

The lines of the court

The baseline marks the back of the
court. The center mark identifies the
middle point of the court. Sidelines run
perpendicular to the net: the inner
sidelines mark off the singles court and
the outer ones, the doubles court. The
area between these two lines is called
the doubles alley, or the tramline area.
The service box is used for singles and
doubles, and indicates where the serve
is to be placed.

Court overview

Occasionally throughout the book
you will see this diagram, which is
used to show different shots and
positions that may be used.

court surfaces

Balls usually bounce lower on faster surfaces such as grass, and higher on slower surfaces such as clay. Big servers and serve-and-volley players (those who serve and then immediately run in to the net to volley) usually prefer fast courts, because shorter points are easier on fast surfaces. Baseliners (see pages 142–43) tend to prefer slower surfaces, as they are more suited to longer points.

a Saving time
On clay courts, you can slide into a shot, which saves time running to hit the ball. Sliding helps balance and can reduce the distance you need to cover on each point.

b Predicting bounce
On a hard court, medium to fast, low bounces keep rallies short, so powerful, hard-serving players have a slight advantage.

c Court preparation
Before play, clay courts are smoothed for a truer ball bounce and to erase marks that the ball has made.

a

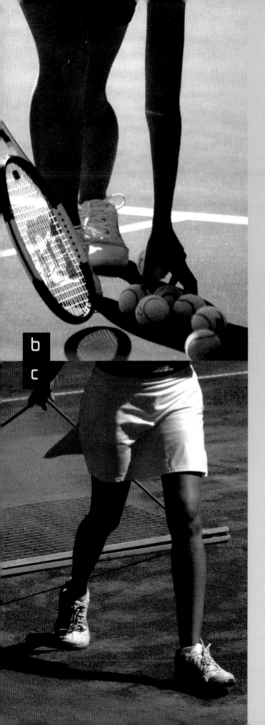

b

c

On fast surfaces

• String your racquet tighter. Because the court is producing more pace, having tighter strings will help control the ball.

• Because the ball comes through quicker, you will have less time, so shorten your backswing.

• The energy supplied from a fast court will give your shots more pace and to keep the ball in, you must hit lower.

• Be aggressive. Hit the ball harder and aim for the corners. One good shot usually means the end of the point on quick surfaces.

On slow surfaces

• Have your racquet strung at a looser tension. You will now need to supply your own power.

• Lengthen your backswing. To help supply the extra power, especially on higher deep shots, take a bigger backswing and hit through with power and topspin.

• Hit the ball higher over the net. Hitting short on a slow court gives your opponent the chance to attack.

• Be patient and work the point! On slow courts, hit the ball hard, but remember, it takes more shots to get the ball past your opponent and win the point.

game, set, and match

Tennis has a unique scoring system. A player can be on the brink of defeat yet, in a few moments, be on the verge of victory. The scoring system is dynamic, and a close match will have players keenly focused and spectators on the edges of their seats. Any enthusiastic player or fan will agree that a close competitive match is both exciting and intense.

The objectives when playing a tennis match are:
1. Win points to win a game
2. Win games to win a set
3. Win sets to win a match!

What is a point?
• When a player serves, the first player to fail to make a legal return loses the point, and the other player wins the point.
• Every point in competitive play is started with the serve.
• Every point is either won or lost. There are several ways of winning points, the most common ones being by your opponent netting the ball, hitting outside the lines, or being unable to get the ball back over the net before the second bounce.

What is a game?

- A game is a series of points. Players start each game at love.
- Love = 0; 1 point = 15; 2 points = 30; 3 points = 40; 4 points = game.
- When each player has three points (40-all), the score is deuce. Players need two consecutive points from deuce to win the game. Winning the point gives the advantage; if followed by a second winning point, the game is won, but if followed by a losing point, the score returns to deuce again.

What is a set?

- A set is a series of games. A player must win six games (being at least two games ahead) to win the set.
- If the score is five games all, two consecutive games are needed to win the set. At six games all, a tie-breaker is played to decide the set.
- The player whose turn it was to serve in the set serves the first point of the tie-break. Their opponent serves the next two points and after that, the serve rotates after every two further points. Players change ends after every six points.
- A tie-breaker is won when a player wins seven points by a margin of two-points or more. When the score is six-all, play continues until a player has a two-point lead, in which case the set is won by seven games to six.

What is a match?

- A match is the best of three sets. A player can win two sets to love or two sets to one. Men's singles matches may go to five sets, the winner being the first to win three sets.

basic rules

Rules are needed for structure and to allow players to compete on an even basis. For most beginners, the rules and system of scoring can seem a bit confusing at first, so learn them as soon as you can to get you started.

It's really quite simple; you have to win more points than your opponent to beat them. Each point starts when one player serves. If the ball bounces in your opponent's service box but they can't reach it, the server gets a point. If the serve is returned, the point continues until someone makes a mistake.

During competitive play

You can use hand signals (along with a call) to indicate whether the ball was in or out. Holding your hand palm down indicates that your opponent's shot was in. Pointing indicates that the ball was out. Pointing to the side means the ball was wide (see left) and pointing up that the ball was long.

During points, the player can make contact with the ball before it bounces. If contact is made after the bounce, the ball must be on or within the perimeter lines of the singles or doubles court to be allowed. A ball cannot be called "out" until it has bounced.

Players must change ends after the first game and then after every odd-numbered game throughout the set. The player who received last in the previous set begins serving in the next. Whoever started serving in a tie-breaker receives in the first game of the following set.

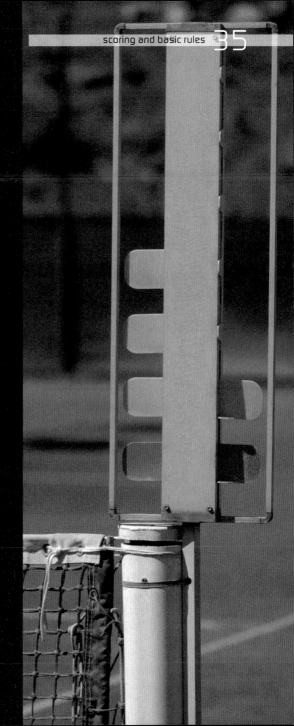

Rules for serving:
• The serve must be played to the diagonal service box.

• Each game starts on the deuce court, and then alternates from side to side with each point played. The server must stand behind the baseline and between the center mark and the singles sideline for singles or the outer sideline for doubles. The feet cannot touch the line or the court before the ball is struck.

• The server has two chances to get the serve inside the service box. When the serve is made, the point begins. If the ball lands inside the box, the point continues. If the serve misses, it is called a fault. Two faults are a double fault, which ends the point.

• When the ball hits the net and lands inside the service box, it is called a let, and that serve is played again.

Rules for returning:
• The receiver can position themselves anywhere, but ideally near the baseline and sideline on the diagonal side from the server.

• The receiver must let the ball bounce inside the service box before playing the ball or the point is lost.

• The receiving player must not deliberately distract the server.

go learn the basics

coming up...

Getting started: 40–55

Mastering the basics means [   ] to grips with the serve, g[   ] strokes, and net play, practicing the ready position, and knowing how and when to step. Learn exactly how the ball responds to your shots, and you'll be ready to get out on the court and enjoy your practice to the full.

Making practice fun: 56–59

Joining a tennis club is your first step toward enjoying regular, relaxed practice with like-minded people of all levels of ability. When you're ready, you can set your[   ]ther challenges and prep[   ] those first friendly singles and doubles matches.

On the court: 60–67

The thrill of a competitive match has players coming back for more. An exciting close match, chasing down good shots and playing great shots of your own, brings out the best in most players. Doubles matches allow you to share the fun with a partner.

the serve

The serve starts every point in a match, and the server is considered to have an advantage.

This is partly because you have two chances to get your serve in, and partly because you can take your time to set up the shot and therefore put your opponents at a disadvantage. They don't know where you are going to place the shot and therefore have to react quickly. Practice to develop an accurate, reliable serve you can repeat over and over again.

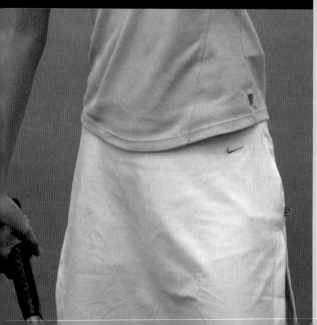

a Prepare
Make the service grip by holding the racquet with your forefinger knuckle on the second bevel. You should be able to extend the racquet to form an almost straight line with your arm.

b Serve it up
To begin the serve, stand just behind the baseline near the center mark, and take a sideways position. Bounce the ball a few times in preparation to serve.

c Take the shot
Toss the ball high and swing the racquet using a throwing motion, making contact with the ball at the top of your reach.

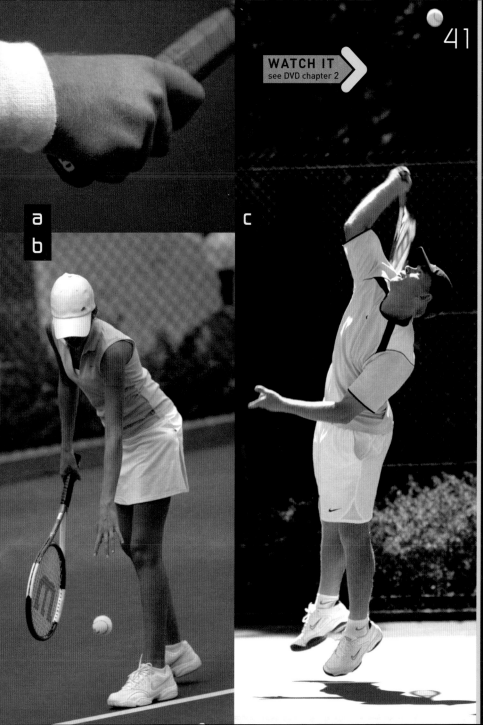

WATCH IT
see DVD chapter 2

Groundstrokes are the basic shots you make once the point has begun.

Although these shots can be played from anywhere in the court, they are usually played from near the baseline and after the ball has bounced.

groundstrokes and grips

How you hold the racquet determines how you play the game, so practice your swing and getting your grip correct until you feel comfortable playing these groundstrokes.

• Shots on the forehand side are made with the swing arm moving alongside and away from the body before swinging forward to play the ball.

• Shots on the backhand side are made with the swing arm taking the racquet back across the front side of the body before swinging forward to play the ball.

• Two-handed backhand players use a combination of these swings.

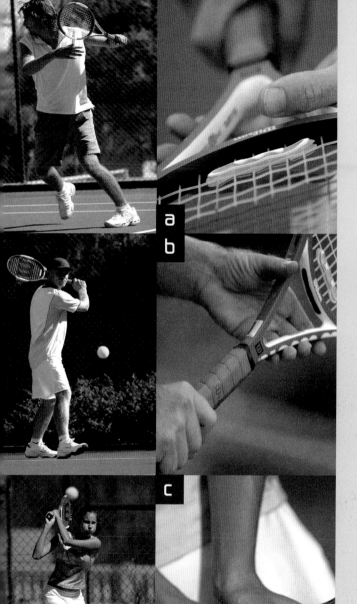

a Forehand grip
For the forehand grip, place the forefinger knuckle anywghere on or betweenbetween the third and fourth bevel of the handle.

b Backhand grip
The correct grip, not strength, affects your ability to use a one-handed backhand. Place the forefinger knuckle on the top bevel for topspin and on the second bevel for underspin. Support the racquet by the throat with the other hand between shots.

c Two-handed backhand grip
For the two-handed backhand grip, take the serve grip by placing your forefinger knuckle on the second bevel. Then place your other hand above it.

net play

Net play involves making contact with the ball close to the net before or immediately after it has bounced. To win consistently from the net, a player needs athletic movement, quick reflexes, and superb accuracy—and two different types of shot to call upon: the volley, and the smash. The volley is any shot hit before the ball bounces; a half-volley is a ball hit just after the bounce. The smash is an attacking shot used when returning a lob (see pages 124–25).

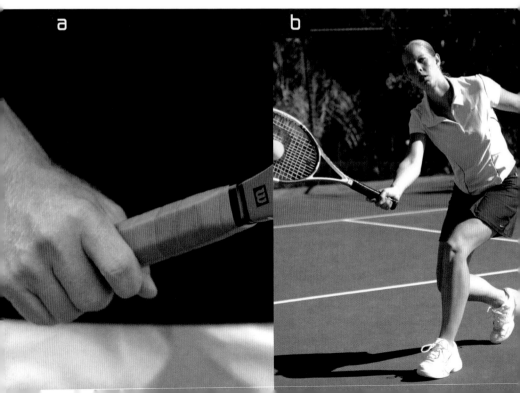

a

b

a Volley grip
To make the correct grip for net play, place your forefinger knuckle on the second bevel of the racquet handle.

b Forehand volley
To play a forehand volley, you'll need a short, compact swing. When the contact is higher, hit it aggressively to the open court. When the ball is lower, hit it deep or use angles.

c Backhand volley
You need to practice the backhand volley to become a complete net player. For a more controlled backhand volley, use one hand at contact to play the shot.

d Smash
The smash should be played when the ball is well above head height. This shot can be played moving forward when the ball is short or backward when the ball is deep. It should be played with power and aimed to the open court.

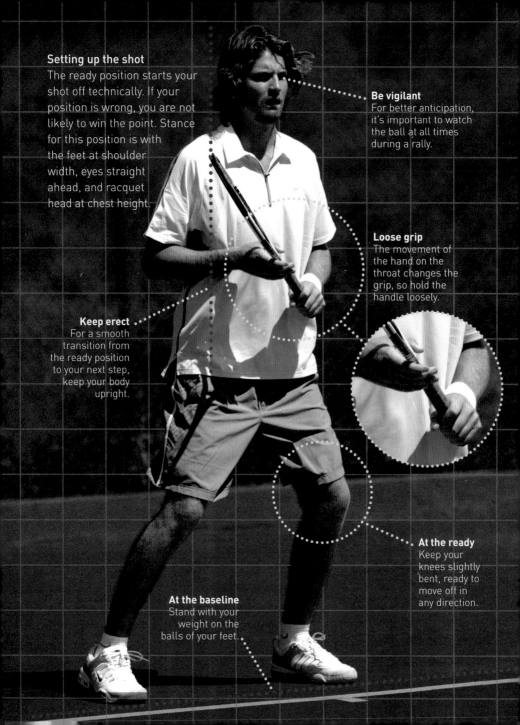

Setting up the shot
The ready position starts your shot off technically. If your position is wrong, you are not likely to win the point. Stance for this position is with the feet at shoulder width, eyes straight ahead, and racquet head at chest height.

Be vigilant
For better anticipation, it's important to watch the ball at all times during a rally.

Loose grip
The movement of the hand on the throat changes the grip, so hold the handle loosely.

Keep erect
For a smooth transition from the ready position to your next step, keep your body upright.

At the ready
Keep your knees slightly bent, ready to move off in any direction.

At the baseline
Stand with your weight on the balls of your feet.

the ready position

The ready position is fundamental to tennis. It gets your body set up to return serve, play groundstrokes, and make volleys. The ready position is taken before and after each shot, and is invaluable as it allows you to push off to the ball with maximum acceleration in as short a time as possible. This position also makes it easier to change to the required grip.

To adopt the ready position, stand just behind the baseline, roughly in the middle of the court. You will need to adjust your court position after each shot when playing competitive points. The ready-position grip is the same as the service grip (see pages 40–41). Hold the racquet with your forefinger knuckle on the second bevel and your other hand on the throat. When you need to use the two-handed backhand, slide your other hand down on to the handle.

You need a stable ready position to return the ball effectively. Face the net and hold your racquet centrally, so you are prepared to return a shot to either your forehand (see far left) or backhand (see left) side.

Many players swing from side to side or bounce while in the ready position. This keeps the mind and body alert and signals to your opponent that you are ready to anticipate their shot.

stepping

For successful shot-making, you must take a step during the backswing. Stepping positions you to take the best possible swing at the ball. You can step in any direction you choose, but remember to tailor your stance to the oncoming ball. The correct stance will ensure that you are able to play the ball successfully and with enough power and accuracy to challenge your opponent and win points.

a An open stance
In this stance, the back leg is out to the side at the top of the backswing. It is mainly used for shots out wide on the forehand side.

b A tactical stance
To be quick and make the best returns against a strong server, use an open stance on either the forehand or the backhand side.

WATCH IT
see DVD chapter 5

c A sideways stance
You are better able to reach balls that are played either short or deep when the legs are positioned in line toward the net.

d A closed stance
This is when the front leg is across the back leg. It is the opposite of an open stance and is mostly used on the backhand side.

Balance and power
The amount that you need to bend as you step varies with the height of contact. Make sure you transfer your weight correctly in order to keep your balance, be steady, and make the most of the shot.

Good contact
Because you are swinging from a solid base, you can make good, firm contact with the ball

Balance
Keep your arm outstretched for better balance while you are making contact with the ball

Early contact
Because the leg stays back, you can swing through and make early contact with the ball

Good swing
When you transfer your weight onto your front leg, you're able to rotate your hips and shoulders forward, producing a powerful forward swing

Hit hard
When making contact with a ball at shoulder level or above, lean forward as you transfer your weight. This will enable you to hit the ball hard using a lower trajectory

bending and weight transfer

How much you bend your legs while stepping and the amount of weight transfer you make after you step are important aspects of an effective shot. This needs to be a smooth action to help you keep your balance.

When going for a low shot, it is important to bend as you move. Whenmoving for your opponent's high shot you will not need to bend so much. To make your shots more effective, you must swing from a solid base, which means having most of your weight over one leg. To achieve this, move your body just after the step, shifting your weight onto that leg. This is called weight transfer.

a Get ready
When stepping forward to play a low forehand, bend your knees. This will allow you to make a low-to-high shot for topspin.

b Shift weight
As you swing around, transfer most of your body weight onto your front leg in order to power the swing.

a

b

adding spin

The rate at which a ball rotates, or spins, has a considerable effect on how it travels through the air and bounces. Putting spin on the ball gives you control over your shots, improving your tennis even further. Spin produces different effects, so you need to learn when and how to use it to best advantage.

- Topspin allows you to hit the ball higher over the net. It pulls the ball down into the court, so you can hit it harder but still keep the ball in play.

- Underspin makes the ball "float," giving you more time to get back in position. When the ball has a lower trajectory it will skid through after it has bounced.

- Sidespin causes the ball to curve in the opposite direction of the racquet path. A ball that curves directly into the body is difficult to return.

Topspin

To create topspin, position yourself behind the ball. Swing through the ball from low to high. The ball will rotate away from you after making contact.

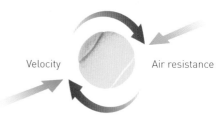

Velocity   Air resistance

Underspin

To create underspin, position yourself beside the ball. Swing through the ball from high to low. The ball will rotate toward you after making contact.

Velocity   Air resistance

Sidespin

Sidespin is mostly used on shots at shoulder level or above. Get behind your shot and start your forward swing at the same level as the ball. Lean forward into contact and hit hard.

Air resistance

Velocity

ball flight

Implementing the correct flight path of the ball over the net and into your opponent's court will improve your tennis immediately. Many players believe, possibly after watching tennis on TV, that the ball is hit very low over the net. Imitating this often leads to frustration and disappointment. To increase your enjoyment, play the ball over the net with a safety margin. For normal baseline rallies, keep the ball roughly head-height over the net. Your consistency level will rise dramatically and your shots will land with more depth.

From the baseline

Baseline play should involve hitting the ball up and over the net with a margin of safety. Constantly playing the ball just over the net is asking for trouble.

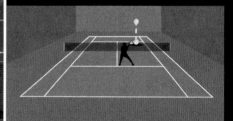

From overhead

When you are making contact with a ball that's high and closer to the net, hit it downward. You now have the margin for error to hit hard and flat.

From low down

When you are close to the net playing a low ball, you will need to hit the ball up. To be successful you must take the pace off the ball and play either a delicate shot just over the net, or hit it high and deep.

A club with a lively social calendar will encourage you to play more, and being around other players motivates you to improve your game.

Joining a tennis club involves paying a monthly or annual fee for the use of the facilities, which vary from club to club. Membership includes the use of the tennis courts, possibly a restaurant, gym, and swimming pool.

Most clubs have a resident tennis pro or tennis coordinator to help members find suitable practice partners. It is important to practice with someone of your own ability, because you can learn and improve together without feeling intimidated by more advanced players. Tennis coaches can also help you to improve many aspects of your game. Of course, being around better players inspires your game, and it's a great boost to your confidence when you find that you can play on equal terms with someone who used to defeat you.

joining a club

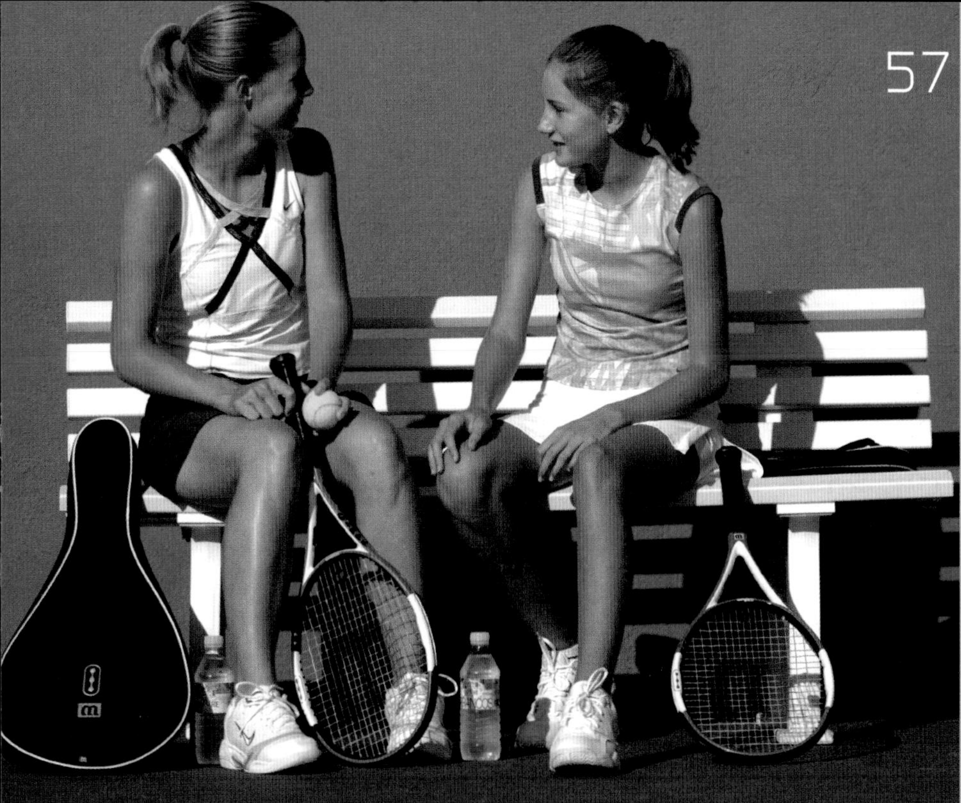

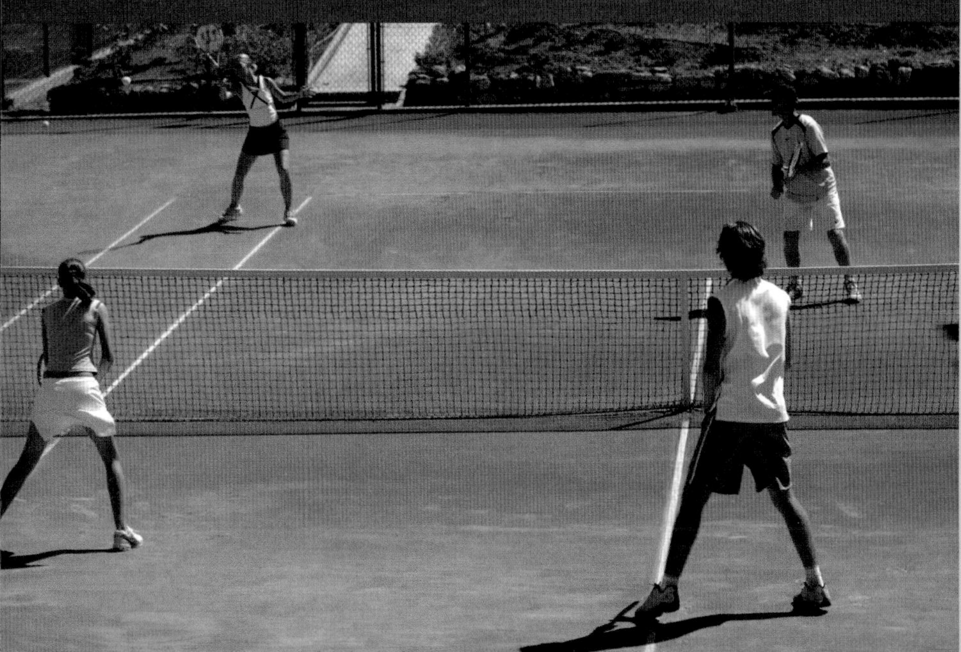

your first practice session

Your first friendly practice session should be fun; for each player, tennis is fun in a different way.

Some players enjoy the social side of the game, others play to get a good workout, while many enjoy the competitive side of the sport. It is helpful to form a "team" with another person and work together to improve your game. When you begin to practice, start off with frequent but short sessions. Build your stamina and skills at the same time.

Tips for practice sessions

Here are some practice drills that you and your partner can use to improve your game:

- Concentrate on getting the ball over the net and building up a rally with your partner.

- Begin each rally by dropping the ball and playing an easy shot to your partner.

- Gently hit each ball to one another and focus on keeping the ball in play.

- Set each other a goal during each practice session; to hit 10 balls inside the court...then 20...then 30.

- To get a taste for competitive play, feed the ball in and play first to eleven points. The winner must be two points ahead when the score reaches 10 all.

- Using a basket of balls, take turns feeding single balls in succession to your partner to simulate a ball machine.

- Practice a few serves at the end of each session to get acquainted with the motion. With steady practice, you will become a better server.

WATCH IT
see DVD chapter 1

what is singles?

Most people start out playing singles, a game in which one player competes against another, using the singles area of the court. When you start out, singles games are about practice and enjoyment. Everyone plays better and learns more when they are relaxed, so enjoy yourself and encourage your playing partner.

To become a good singles player, you must have a certain level of fitness, a variety of shots, and a knowledge of strategy. When you've practiced your basic shots and your rallying is improving (see pages 112–13), play some competitive points using the serve. Although you are playing friendly points, it's always nice to win, so when you are more in control of your shots, try to place them away from your partner.

Here are some useful tips to remember when you are playing singles:

- Go back to the ready position after each shot you play (see pages 46-47).

- To keep your opponent from dominating the points, play your groundstrokes as deep as possible.

- For longer and more exciting points, learn to serve and return with consistency.

- For better movement and to raise the level of your entire game, be light on your feet—you will reach more shots.

- Get all your serves in deep—this puts pressure on your opponent.

- For a consistently solid contact, keep your eyes on the ball.

- Play the ball down the lines (near either sideline), then change your tactics and play cross court.

- Visualize your shots as you hit them—mental pictures produce physical results.

- Buy time at every opportunity so that you can prepare yourself properly for the next shot.

playing singles

Now that you are becoming more confident, it's time to play a friendly, competitive match—and look forward to that exciting adrenalin rush. A simple tip for consistency is to play most of your shots crosscourt. The net at the middle is lower and the court is longer, giving you a greater margin to play the ball hard and inside the lines.

The basic rules of the game are simple (see pages 32–35). Play someone at a similar level as yourself so you can be sure to get an exciting and challenging game. Decide who will begin the match by spinning the racquet. The other player calls "up" or "down," before the racquet lands on the court. Confirm the winner by checking the logo on the end of the handle. The winner elects to serve or return; the opponent chooses which end they will start from. Always start your match with a positive attitude.

When you are playing a friendly singles match, remember these golden rules:

• Acknowledge your opponent's good shots.

• To save confusion, the server should call out the score before each serve.

• Give 100 percent of your effort and concentration.

• Be competitive but friendly; always give your opponent the benefit of close line calls.

• Shake hands at the end of the match. The loser congratulates the winner. Afterward, discuss the match and arrange a rematch.

what is doubles?

Being a good singles player does not always mean that you will be good at doubles, which demands different skills and brings different pressures. Doubles has the same basic rules and scoring as singles. In doubles, four players use the entire marked court. A doubles team comprises two players who work in tandem to try to out-play and outwit the opposing team.

Doubles teams can be composed of two men, two women, or a mixed team. Although it is played against the same combination in competitive matches, in non-competitive matches, other combinations can be decided on the basis of players' strengths. Doubles is a social game and club players usually change partners to enhance the social atmosphere. Always choose a compatible partner for competitive play. Good communication is important, and you should feel relaxed enough to have fun. Keeping the same partner is a big advantage for competitions.

Skills to dominate in doubles

• Communication is key in doubles. When the ball from your opponents is down the middle, call "mine" if you have the best chance to play a good shot, or call "yours" if your partner has the best opportunity.

• Advanced doubles play requires sharp volleying skills and a good serve.

• Only one player is allowed to hit each shot. If your partner touches the ball after you have hit it, the point is won by your opponents.

• You need to be accurate since you have two opponents ready to pounce. Doubles is a fast game, so quick reactions are vital.

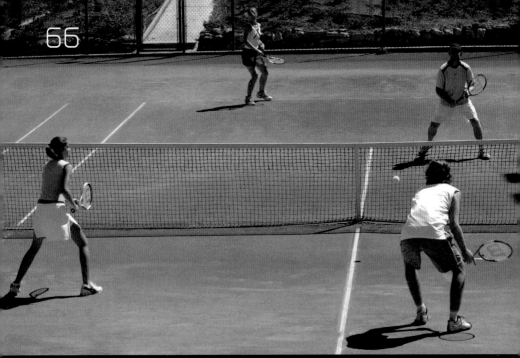

playing doubles

Doubles requires great teamwork—the best players seem to be able to read each other's minds. Once you have been playing with the same partner for a while, you will find that you can anticipate their moves. You need to work on your team strategy in order to control the net, as doubles is really a net game; a baseline game will not win you as many matches as a good net game. Doubles players also need to develop their volley, and the best place to hit the ball to is deep and down the middle or an angle out wide.

Court positioning for doubles has no set rules, but ideally the formation of each team should be one up, one back. When a team is serving, the server stands behind the baseline between the doubles sideline and the center mark, while their partner is positioned at the net. When a team is returning, the player who is returning the serve is at the baseline and their partner is positioned at the net. You need to be aware at all times of where your partner is and where your opponents are.

Tips for playing doubles

• Each player in a doubles team should cover half of the court. After deciding which team will serve first, that team should let the strongest server begin. The strongest returner should take the ad side.

• When returning, hit the ball cross-court away from your opponent at the net.

• To keep the opposition on the run, hit the ball down their doubles alley or over their heads.

• Players at the net should take any weak ball within range and make a winning shot.

• Be aggressive at the net, and don't be afraid to make mistakes. Even if you hit long or wide, your opponents will be unnerved by your presence at the net.

• The key to better volleys is to keep it simple, with very little backswing.

• Work out a signals system with your partner to communicate your intentions—here (see left), the player indicates which way he wants the serve to go.

go play

coming up...

Enhancing the serve: 72–75

The serve starts the point, and gives the server an edge for the rest of the point, so it's vital to develop a technically sound service motion. In this section, learn how to power your serve and use the kick serve and slice serve to your advantage.

Improving ground play: 76–83

The majority of shots are played from the baseline, so to become a tough opponent, you must master groundstrokes. Most players attack their opponent's backhand side, keeping the ball away from their stronger forehand. Developing a powerful backhand deprives your opponent of easy points.

Mastering net play: 84–89

To be a versatile player, you need to play shots from all around the court. You can easily win more points by sharpening your net skills—so here's how to move in and take the ball early.

Moving like a pro: 90–103

Your biggest weapon against opponents is to be quick chasing down their best shots and placing them back into court. Learning to move effectively will enhance the shots you play and greatly improve your entire game.

powering the serve

A player has two chances to start the point and play the serve into the diagonal service box. Hit the first serve with power to gain an advantage, but play it safe with the second serve. A great serve is your first chance at winning every point, so the more force you get behind it, the better. Consistency is the key, so practice it as much as you can.

1 Stand sideways just behind the baseline and place your feet shoulder-width apart. Toss the ball with a straight arm.

2 Keeping your shoulders turned sideways, hold the swing and extend your toss arm up high.

3 Start your swing by raising your racquet, bending your arm to 90°, and lifting your forearm to vertical. Swing slowly and bend your legs.

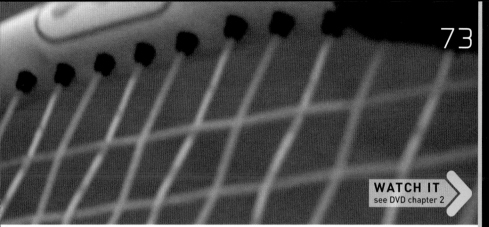

WATCH IT
see DVD chapter 2

4 In a continuous motion, drop the racquet behind your back, push off with your legs and get your swing elbow up by rolling your shoulders forward. Keep your head up, reach high, and accelerate into contact with the ball, imparting as much power as you can to the shot.

5 The toss arm will have traveled across your body during contact. After contact, land on your front foot inside the baseline and get to the ready position (see page 47) as quickly as possible. The follow-through goes down and in front of your body.

types of serve

There are three types of serve: the kick serve, the slice serve, and the flat serve. All three can be used as either the first or second serve, but the basic serve strategy is to use the flat or slice as a first serve—the flat serve imparts pace and the slice takes your opponent out of position—and the kick serve, which is the safest of the three, as a second serve. It is important to vary your choice of serve to enhance the effectiveness of your play.

a Kick serve
Used to clear the net safely and bounce high, the kick is awkward to return. Toss the ball back and across for the low-to-high swing action and make contact almost behind the head.

b Slice serve
The slice is used mainly to make the ball move away from your opponent, forcing them to reach. Toss the ball in front and in line with your swing shoulder. Imagine swinging around the outside edge of the ball.

Flat serve
The flat serve uses very little spin and is used to produce pace so your opponent has less time to react. Toss the ball above your head and forward into court, and hit the ball squarely in front of your body.

Vertical slant
Shoulders are slanted to get your swing arm to a vertical position at contact.

More power
Flex the wrist into contact for extra acceleration and power

Ball contact
Your arm goes across your body as you make contact with the ball.

To the front
The follow-through goes down and in front of your body.

Balance
Because the body is leaning forward into the serve, you need to raise your back leg for balance.

WATCH IT
see DVD chapter 2

perfecting the forehand

The forehand is the most used shot in tennis, and the one that most people learn first. With practice, it can be developed into a useful weapon. Play the forehand with topspin and use it aggressively, dictating play from the baseline. This is a major groundstroke for both beginner and advanced player alike, and perfecting it will greatly improve your game.

1 From the ready position, make a half-turn sideways and adopt a forehand grip (see page 43). At the same time, place the racquet on the flat palm of your other hand

2 .Begin the backswing, keeping your arm bent. Slightly lift your racquet and make a circular swing. Swing slowly and rotate your shoulders.

3 Continue to swing slowly, placing the racquet below the level of the oncoming ball to lift the ball and impart topspin.

WATCH IT
see DVD chapter 3

4 Swing from low to high and accelerate into contact, watching the ball onto the racquet, and hitting it hard. Keep your back leg from coming forward and, unless the ball is low, push off and rise up into the shot.

5 Follow through across your body, and let the swing pull you back to the ready position in preparation to play your next shot.

When it is played correctly, the two-handed backhand is a dominant shot, as it allows you to attack.

You can play the shot on the rise—in its upward trajectory—which enables you to stand inside the baseline and take the ball early. Low shots and shots above the shoulders can be hit aggressively. You can also disguise the direction of the shot and wrongfoot your opponent.

a stronger two-handed backhand

The two-handed backhand is a versatile shot that gives extra strength and control, especially for novice players.

- Topspin lobs (see pages 124–25) can be played with ease and to great effect.

- Even when the shot is hit late, you can still keep the ball in play.

- A two-handed swing gives you control when returning a powerful serve.

WATCH IT
see DVD chapter 4

1 Begin with one hand on the racquet handle and the other on the neck.

2 Make a half-turn sideways and bring your other hand down onto the handle.

3 Begin putting your weight onto your back leg and slowly start to take the racquet back.

4 Keeping your hands held down, complete your backswing and shoulder rotation. Drop your racquet below the level of the oncoming ball.

5 Watch the ball and make sure you accelerate into contact, keeping your front leg well forward.

6 Follow through across your body and over your shoulder. Let the finish pull you face-on to your opponent.

one-handed backhand with topspin

The key to a more powerful one-handed topspin backhand is to play the ball at waist level. This ensures that you can give the ball topspin by swinging from low to high, thereby ensuring power with maximum control. Play this shot when the ball is hit to the opposite of your forehand side. Not only is it a very reliable groundstroke, but top players also use it as an overwhelmingly aggressive attacking weapon.

1 From the ready position, watch the ball carefully and when you see it coming to your backhand side, prepare to move.

2 Turn almost sideways and adopt a backhand grip (see page 43). Hold the racquet throat with your fingertips and make sure the racquet head is up.

3 With your arm slightly bent and keeping your hand low, take your racquet back slowly. Turn your shoulders while making your backswing.

WATCH IT
see DVD chapter 4

4 Swing forward slowly and lower your hand beneath the level of the oncoming ball. The racquet head should be behind your body as your arm straightens.

5 Accelerate into contact, making sure to stay sideways while keeping your other arm back. Swing from low to high, imparting topspin.

6 The follow-through goes higher than shoulder level. Your arm extends, and the racquet head goes above your wrist.

a better backhand slice

Perfecting the slice is a good way to develop better attacking and defensive skills. It's most effective on fast courts because the ball skids through at speed. Because the shot gives you a long reach, use it when you have been taken out wide. The backhand slice is particularly effective when playing shots above shoulder height, as they can be played assertively. The shot can be used when the ball is low and short, and can be hit hard or with touch.

1 Turn sideways and lift the racquet head to almost vertical. Keep the ready-position grip and place the thumb of your other hand over the frame of the racquet for maximum control.

2 Slowly begin to take the racquet back and up. Keep your swing arm bent and watch the ball. For a slice shot, move into a position beside the ball.

3 To complete the backswing, raise your hand above the ball and position your racquet horizontally.

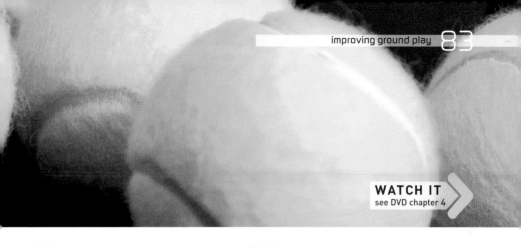

WATCH IT
see DVD chapter 4

4 Swing out to the side using a high-to-low action to impart backspin. Watch the ball into contact, accelerate, and stay sideways. Don't let your back leg and arm come forward.

5 The follow-through is a down-to-up U-shaped motion, with the racquet face opening skyward.

effective forehand volleying

When you have learned the forehand volley, you can put away your opponent's easy shots and keep them under pressure.

The volley—any shot that is hit before the ball bounces—is used in the forecourt with a short high-to-low swing. The half-volley is played just after the ball has bounced. When it is played from the front of the court, be sure to use a short low-to-high swing.

A volley using a groundstroke shot is called a swinging volley. These shots are played around midcourt when your opponent has made a weak "moon ball" shot (an extremely high lob). When you feel confident with your groundstrokes, step in and play an aggressive swinging volley to the open court.

1 Have an aggressive mind-set and be ready to move closer to the net when your opponent's shot is weak.

WATCH IT
see DVD chapter 6

Adjust your swing
A high forehand volley should be hit hard and placed away from your opponent (see right).

A half-volley should be hit more softly and placed deeper into the court on your opponent's backhand side (see far right).

2 Make a half-turn, keeping the racquet head above your wrist. Release your other hand from the racquet.

3 Stretch out with your swing arm while moving your other arm to the side. Keep the racquet head up, step across, and watch the ball into contact.

4 The forward swing is short and accelerated using a slight high-to-low action. Make a short follow-through with the racquet face opening.

backhand volleying

For better backhand volleys, move into a position beside the ball while making the shot. The key point to remember is to use a small high-to-low swing to strike the ball—straighten your arm as you make contact, and use minimal follow-through.

1 From the ready position, turn almost sideways and lift the racquet head to nearly vertical.

• Most players focus on their forehand volleys. To cover the net effectively, practice your backhand volley equally.

• Play your first volley inside the service line, then move closer to the net for the second—this gives your opponent less reaction time and allows you to play acute angles.

• For drop volleys, hit just over the net. You'll need to take the pace off the ball, so open the racquet face as the ball makes contact with the strings.

WATCH IT
sée DVD chapter 6

Volley technique

For high volleys, use a big swing, dropping the racquet head further back the higher you swing (see far left).

For low volleys, use a short swing. For a half-volley, use a short low-to-high swing (see left).

2 Stretch to the side and keep the racquet head up and the face open. Start to bring your front leg forward, or across if contact is made out wide.

3 Step forward or across and watch the ball into contact. The forward swing is accelerated and short, using a high-to-low action.

4 Make a short follow-through, allowing the racquet face to open up gradually.

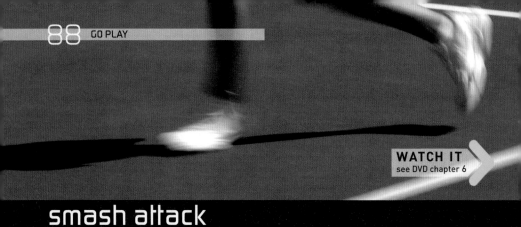

WATCH IT
see DVD chapter 6

smash attack

Make every effort to smash when your opponent plays a lob, as a good smash is difficult to return and can earn you a valuable point. After taking the shot, move into the net to keep them on the defensive. As this shot is usually played in the front half of the court, hit it with power. If made from a deep position, place your smash accurately. If the ball is very high, let it bounce, then play the shot.

1 Forehand smash
From the ready position, turn sideways and watch the ball closely.

2 Move quickly and position yourself under the ball, bringing your swing arm alongside your body.

3 Slowly move your forearm to vertical, and reach up with your other arm.

1 **Backhand smash**
From the ready position, turn sideways. With your hand at shoulder level, drop the racquet head. Shift your weight back.

2 Spring up to the ball and rotate your shoulders into contact. Straighten your arm and for extra power use your wrist..

3 You will land with your back to your opponent, so move into the ready position quickly.

4 Swing slowly and drop the racquet head behind your back. Move your elbow up and shoulders forward.

5 Be aggressive! Keep your head up, reach high, and accelerate into contact.

6 After contact, the follow-through should go across your body.

split-step and return

The split-step is an advanced and dynamic ready position that allows you to move quickly for a shot in any direction. It is particularly useful when you are preparing to return a serve.

A split-step position involves separating your feet more than shoulder-width apart and bending your knees with your body relaxed and upright. This position is taken during play when your opponent is making their forward swing and is about to contact the ball. For general baseline play, you simply go into the split-step from wherever you are as your opponent hits the ball.

1 While you are waiting to return serve, crouch and shift your weight from side to side.

2 When your opponent starts their service motion and is nearing contact, stand upright and begin to take a step forward.

3 In one continuous movement, bring the other foot alongside and hop forward, separating your feet.

WATCH IT
see DVD chapter 5

WATCH IT
see DVD chapter 5

split-step and volley

Although all areas of play need the split-step, it is especially important when you are moving in to volley. When you are running forward, it is very difficult to change direction. Although doing a split-step slows you down slightly, it enables you to move off to whichever side the ball is coming from. Employing this step also gives you long reach on both sides, and enables you to employ effective volleying techniques (see pages 84–87).

1 Take a step forward as your opponent swings at the ball. Bring your other foot up alongside and hop forward, separating your feet.

2 Move immediately after making the split-step—don't hold the position—it's important not to be static before moving off for the volley.

3 From the split-step position, you can move quickly to both your forehand and backhand sides.

side-step and forehand

Side-stepping gives you speed and accuracy. It is an essential part of good footwork, and helps you to move freely and smoothly toward the ball. To side-step, you simply bring one foot up to the other, then step away. Before moving backward for a deep shot, forward for a short shot, or to the side, turn sideways and employ side-steps.

1 After making your split-step, turn your back foot in the direction of your forehand side.

2 Make a small bouncy side-step to your other foot. At the same time, start your backswing.

3 Keep your weight back and rotate your shoulders as you make your step and backswing.

WATCH IT
see DVD chapter 5

4 Bend your legs
as you step out to
the side. Because
you are playing a
forehand, use an
open stance.

5 Transfer all your weight
onto your front leg and
start your forward swing.

6 Make an accelerated
low-to-high swing
into contact, and
rise up to help you
follow through.

side-step and backhand

Using the side-step effectively on the backhand creates free-flowing movement into the shot, and gives you controlled power with little effort. It also gives you the ability to uncoil into the hit with perfect timing. Make sure you give yourself plenty of room to swing out and up as you step forward to meet the ball.

1 After the split-step, start to lean in the direction of your backhand side.

2 Make a short bouncy side-step to your other foot, turning your hips and shoulders. Hold the backswing until the ball is approaching you.

3 Step out to the side with your back leg and begin your backswing. Put all your weight onto that leg before stepping across.

WATCH IT
see DVD chapter 5 >

4 Now continue to make the backswing as you step across with your front leg.

5 Transfer your weight onto your front leg while you make your forward swing.

6 Rise up to allow a long and smooth follow-through.

a b

crossover steps

A crossover step is when one leg goes up to and across the other leg. The step can be used equally successfully whether playing backhand or forehand. When moving sideways, use it in place of the side-step when you need to cover the court quickly. Because the crossover uses fewer, bigger steps, it is particularly effective when chasing down good shots out wide. Basically, you are leaping across the court to get yourself into the right area to receive the ball.

a Turn and lean
After the split-step, turn your leading foot in the direction of your backhand side, leaning your body to get started.

b Move across
Keep your eye on the ball and bring your other leg up and across your front leg as the ball approaches you.

Good positioning
The crossover step can be used to get you to exactly where you need to be on the court to make your return, in a good position sideways-on to the ball.

Hold the swing
When taking a big crossover step, you will need to hold your backswing a little longer.

Lean forward
During the crossover, lean forward to launch yourself across the court.

Bend your leg
By bending the leg, you can take a bigger explosive step out wide and cover more of the court.

Best foot forward
The crossover is usually used to travel from one side of the court to the other.

WATCH IT
see DVD chapter 5

Using the crossover step is the best way to negate your opponent's attempt to push you back and away from the net. You can use the crossover step effectively with the forehand smash, when an opponent's lob is deep.

The next time your opponent makes a deep lob, play your smash jumping backward. It is one of the most exhilarating shots in tennis and will leave your opponents wondering just how much better their lobs will need to be.

crossover and smash

WATCH IT
see DVD chapter 5

1 Turn sideways as you begin to move backward.

2 With your front leg, make a big crossover step going backward.

3 You're set to take a big step backward, covering even more court as you prepare for the jump smash.

4 Shift all your weight onto your back leg before pushing off and rising up to meet the ball.

5 Jump as high as you can and hit the ball while you are off the ground.

6 You should land on your other leg and then move back up to the net, remembering to split-step.

recovery steps

Recovery steps get you back in play after retrieving and hitting your opponent's shot. In competitive play, the ready position is not static. Now you should position yourself halfway between your oponent's next possible shots. So, if you hit crosscourt, take recovery steps just before the center mark. A down-the-line shot requires recovery to the other side of center, or around the center mark if hitting down the middle.

1 As soon as you have played a shot that takes you out of position, be ready to react quickly to the next shot.

2 To make a quick start for your recovery, begin by pushing off with your back leg.

3 Lean your body and make a big cross-over step. Be sure to face your opponent while doing so.

WATCH IT
see DVD chapter 5

4 After making the crossover step, go back to the side-step. Prepare for a shot from your opponent to either side of the court.

5 Be bouncy. Both feet should leave the ground so you can make a wider step out and cover more of the court.

6 When your opponent is swinging forward to meet the ball, your last side-step will be a split-step, so you can respond quickly to your opponent's next shot.

go play smarter

coming up...

The early advantage: 108–11

Learning to hit powerful serves and aiming them near the lines gives you an advantage in every match you play. When you can consistently hold your serve, you can take more risks on your returns to break serve.

Sound strategies: 112–17

Before you can apply advanced strategies, you need to form winning game plans. When you learn to rally crosscourt consistently, and select the right shots, you'll lead your opponent to believe that they need to take all the risks to win.

Putting the pressure on: 118–21

Learning to play and win a tennis match requires you to employ a variety of tactics successfully. With these tactics, you can create strategies against your opponent's weaknesses, applying constant pressure.

Keeping your opponent guessing: 122–31

To have an edge over your opponent, you must learn to use a variety of specialized shots. With these shots and an ability to change a losing game plan, your opponent will never have a relaxed moment throughout the match.

WATCH IT
see DVD chapter 8

using your serve

Every point begins with a serve followed by a return, unless the serve is an ace. For this reason, they should be practiced and improved so you can have the early advantage.

The most important thing to do when serving is to avoid serving double faults. Otherwise, the point will be lost without your opponent even hitting the ball. As your confidence grows, you can vary your shot so that you place the ball in different areas of the service box each time. This makes it difficult for your opponent to return, but fault-free serving should come before tactics every time.

Tactics to win your service points

- The sun can restrict vision during service. To minimize the effects, adjust the toss and your service motion.

- Hitting an ace is the best way to win a point. Use the flat serve and aim for the lines.

- For a better chance of acing your opponent or inducing a weak return, vary the serve placement, reducing your opponent's reaction time.

- Make things difficult for your opponent by aiming for either corner of the service box. They will really have to run to return the ball.

- Aim for your opponent's body—they will find it difficult to return the ball because there will be no time to get into position to play the shot.

- Be aware of your opponent's weaknesses. For example, if they have a weak backhand, serve to that side.

- Stay clear of the net. Although you get a second serve, it can be off-putting if you net your first serve.

Plan your shots
Vary the ball placement to keep your opponent guessing. Before serving, decide on tactics. For example, visualize making a slice serve out wide and hitting the weak return to their open court.

returning the serve

WATCH IT
see DVD chapter 8

Good returns can neutralize the server's advantage. For better returns against a strong server use the split-step and an open stance.

To gain an advantage when returning, watch where the server places their ball toss. This provides a clue to the type of serve they will use and allows you to prepare mentally for your return.

Returning strategies

• When returning serve on a faster surface, keep your shots compact. On slower surfaces, you'll have time to take a bigger swing.

• When you face a player with a weak serve, don't let the ball drop. Move forward and take the ball at the top of the bounce.

• Always play an aggressive forehand return when the ball is placed in the middle of the service box.

• When your opponent has a powerful serve, move back to give yourself more time to react. For more control, shorten your backswing.

Eye on the ball
Watching the ball from the time it leaves the server's hand will help you to anticipate where it's going.

Aim low
When facing a serve-and-volley player—one who serves, then runs to the net to volley—step forward and aim at their feet when hitting the return.

Ready position
One-handed backhand players should use the ready position grip (see pages 46–47) and support the racquet at the throat.

Adjust your grip
Two-handed backhanders should keep both hands on the handle when returning serve. This allows you to return with only a small adjustment needed.

rallying

When you keep the ball in play, consistently hitting it over the net, you are participating in a rally. To most players, simply keeping the ball in play doesn't seem like a good enough strategy and they become anxious to end the point early, going for a big shot close to the lines. But rallying is a fundamental strategy of tennis and must be practiced. By rallying and chasing down lots of shots, you will become a tougher opponent. Being consistent and letting your opponent take all the risks is the easiest way to win a match.

Taking the advantage during a rally

- After a serve or return, play your shots crosscourt; your opponent will then have less open court to make you run.

- Aim well inside the lines; if you constantly aim for the lines, you are less likely to keep the ball in play.

- Clear the net with a safe margin; your shots will land deeper, making it harder for your opponent to attack.

- Vary your choice of shot; being predictable allows your opponent to form a winning game plan easily.

a

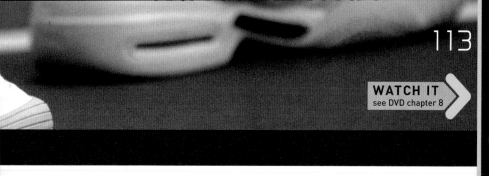

WATCH IT
see DVD chapter 8

a Stepping in
A forehand groundstroke should be used aggressively during a baseline rally. Whenever your opponent hits a weak shot, step in and use the forehand to start your attack.

b Clearing the net
Players with a one-handed backhand should hit the ball with heavy topspin and safely clear the net.

c From the baseline
Practice to develop a strong two-handed backhand, which will allow you to dictate play from the baseline area.

d Out of court
When you are taken out of court, make your shot with a backhand slice to help you float the ball deep across the court.

shot selection

Shot selection involves the type of shot you choose and where you place the ball into your opponent's court. From your range of shots, you need to select the most suitable option to keep the ball in play. This takes the pressure off you and places it back onto your opponent. When on the receiving end of some great tactical play, don't give up—the point is not over. There's always a chance to reverse the pattern of play by selecting the correct shot and placement.

a Short swing
When your opponent's shot is low, use a shorter swing to get under the ball and lift it over the net.

c Safety shot
When the ball is deep and you must move backward, hit your shot high and with depth. Trying to play a winner from this position is called low percentage tennis.

b Block return
When returning against a strong server, block the ball and place the return deep to their backhand side. Your goal is to gradually play yourself into a rally and win the point.

d Quick decision
When the ball is wide, hit it deep crosscourt or high and down the line so you have time to move back into position.

Tips for selecting shots

- When an angled shot takes you out of court, play an angle of your own.

- When chasing a drop shot, lift the ball and place it deep down the line. This cuts down on your opponent's angle, and puts you in a strong position at the net.

- After reaching a difficult lob, place it deep to the opponent's backhand side and move in to the net.

d

WATCH IT
see DVD chapter 8

working the point

Rallying crosscourt keeps you in the point—a simple winning strategy. But when competing against tougher opponents, you will need to employ other tactics and play smarter. This is called working the point.

Forced error
To force your opponent wide, hit the ball mid-court and close to the sidelines, adding pace and topspin.

Weak reply
Aim well inside the lines. The constant pressure of your powerful shots will wear your opponent down and induce a weak reply.

a Advantage

Hit the ball wide, taking your opponent out of court. You are now at an advantage as your opponent must come up with a good shot. If not, play their weak shot to the open court.

b Go faster

Pick up the pace of your shots. This makes it difficult for your opponent to control the ball easily, and when they play a weak shot, you can attack the ball and win the point.

c New tactics

Change the direction of the ball from crosscourt to down the line, making it hard for your opponent to play a good shot. This opens up the court, giving you a chance to use other tactics.

Change direction
To change your play from crosscourt to down the line, play from well inside the sidelines for a better chance of getting the ball in.

WATCH IT
see DVD chapter 8

attacking and defending

When to attack:
- Your opponent hits a short ball in the middle of the court. Hit these balls hard to the open court.

- Using your first serve. Aim close to the lines and hit your serve hard to force a weak return.

- Against an opponent with a weak serve. Stand in before the baseline and take the return early.

When to defend:
- Against an opponent with a big serve. Block the return and place to the server's backhand side.

- You are taken out wide in a baseline rally. Hit the ball high and deep giving you time to move back into play.

Winning against tough opponents is often decided by just a few points. It may seem natural to excel at only one or the other, but in order to win close matches consistently, you need to develop good skills at both attacking and defending.

Attacking is taking advantage of your opponent's weak or badly placed shots. Step in and hit these shots hard in to the open court. When the opportunity for attack is less obvious, put the pressure on by approaching the net or use angled shots to take your opponent out of court. Standing in on a weak second serve shows your intention to be aggressive, which often leads to double faults.

Good placement and running hard to reach well-placed shots are effective defensive skills. This forces your opponent to hit lots of good shots just to win one point. When you attack every weak shot, they will know that playing safe is not good enough and pressure starts to build.

a Attacking
Players must learn to be aggressive when chances arise on the backhand side. If you attack only from the forehand, you are wasting half your opportunities.

b Defending
Even when the ball seems out of reach, make your best effort to get it back into play. Every extra point you win counts toward your score and places pressure on your opponent to play better shots.

In a game of tennis, sometimes you actively win the point, and sometimes you give it away. Winners are shots that your opponent is unable to reach, and can be played anywhere into their court. Unforced errors are unnecessary mistakes. You simply throw away the point without your opponent having to make an effort to win it.

winners and unforced errors

Most winners are made by playing either a hard, deep shot or an angled shot to the open court, both of which are difficult to return. Winning shots can be made at the net using a volley or a smash. These can be impossible to return. They can also be made from a drop shot or a lob. To play better tennis and win more matches, you should aim for a spot in your opponent's court.

Key to success
Concentrate on playing a good game of tennis, rather than rushing to make a winning shot.

- Develop the discipline to aim for a specific area of your opponent's court, regardless of whether or not you think they can return your shot.

- Focus on pace and where the ball is best placed to win the point.

Most matches are won because of a player's excessive unforced errors, rather than a barrage of winners. Players often attempt a winner too early in the point or when the opportunity is simply not there. This, along with a lack of concentration, is the major reason for making unforced errors. Errors of this kind are discouraging, and lead to negative thoughts and poor results. To help guard against making unforced errors, you should hit five shots inside the court before attempting a winning shot.

Angled and dink shots are used to put your opponent into difficult situations, forcing them into higher, weaker shots, which gives you a better chance to win the point.

angled and dink shots

Angled shots are best used when the ball is short and close to the sidelines. They are hit crosscourt and played with topspin, using an arced flight path. This allows you to create sharp-angled shots. To wrongfoot your opponent, hit your angled shot harder and lower using less angle. A well-hit angled shot makes it difficult for your opponent to cover the open court, and often leads to weak replies.

Dinks are soft, dipping shots that can catch your opponent off guard. The trick is to hit the ball low over the net and keep it short, forcing your opponent to lift the ball. Dink shots can often push your opponent into making mistakes; the element of surprise is key here because they will not be expecting a low, short ball with no pace.

WATCH IT
see DVD chapter 7

a Angled shots
When shots are hit with heavy topspin, they can be played shorter into your opponent's court with more angle, pulling your opponent wide.

b Dink shots
To play a dink shot, hit the ball low over the net and place it at your opponent's feet. Do this to an opponent who is moving forward or stationed at the net. Dink shots are hit without much spin, and need accuracy and touch to be successful.

a

b

WATCH IT
see DVD chapter 7

how to lob

When your opponent has taken an aggressive position at the net and passing them is proving difficult, it's time to use the offensive or defensive lob.

Offensive lobs are hit with topspin from around the baseline. Lean back during the forward swing and create a high ball flight. The more topspin you can impart, the faster the ball will drop into the court, which means you can play a deeper lob. Net players often close in after their first volley, and this is an opportune time to use the lob.

Defensive lobs are hit with underspin or very little spin. They are used when the ball is too low, high, or wide, and when topspin is no longer possible. When the ball is low or wide, start the racquet from underneath with an open racquet face. Hit through and up, lifting the ball high and deep—and keeping yourself in the point.

Defensive
When your opponent has you in trouble, hit your lob high and deep. This makes playing a smash out of the air more difficult for them to do safely.

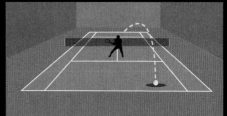

Offensive
For the best chances of making your topspin lob an outright winner, play it from near the baseline and within the singles sidelines.

1 Defensive
Use a volley-type motion, opening the racquet and lifting the ball high and deep over your opponent's backhand side, forcing them back.

2 Be ready to move forward toward the net if your lob goes successfully over your opponent's head.

1 Offensive
Whip the racquet through contact on a steep low-to-high swing path and create heavy topspin.

2 Aim the lob out of reach of your opponent and let the spin dip the ball quickly into the court.

Golden rules

- If playing a defensive lob, aim it over your opponent's backhand side— the backhand smash is the weaker shot.

- Play most of your lobs crosscourt; the court is longer than playing your lob down the line.

- Use the lob when the sun will make it difficult for your opponent to see the ball and make a solid smash.

- Use the lob against the wind; you can play the ball high over your opponent and the wind will help you keep it in. Lobbing with the wind is a difficult shot to control.

- Hide your intention to lob until the last possible moment.

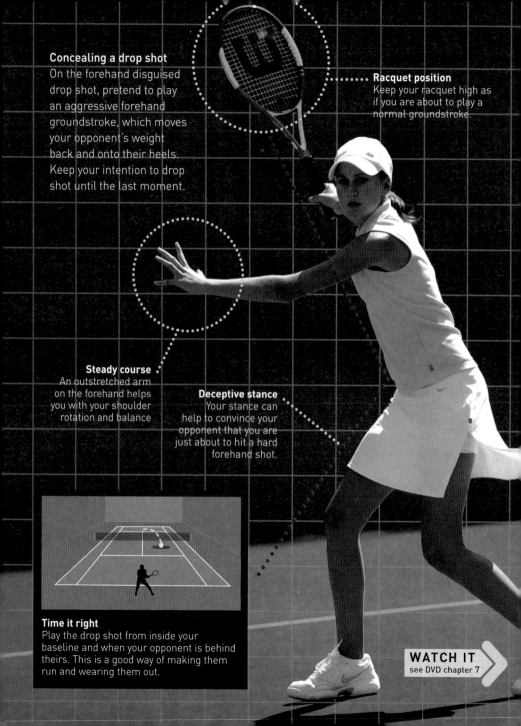

Concealing a drop shot
On the forehand disguised drop shot, pretend to play an aggressive forehand groundstroke, which moves your opponent's weight back and onto their heels. Keep your intention to drop shot until the last moment.

Racquet position
Keep your racquet high as if you are about to play a normal groundstroke.

Steady course
An outstretched arm on the forehand helps you with your shoulder rotation and balance

Deceptive stance
Your stance can help to convince your opponent that you are just about to hit a hard forehand shot.

Time it right
Play the drop shot from inside your baseline and when your opponent is behind theirs. This is a good way of making them run and wearing them out.

WATCH IT
see DVD chapter 7

drop shots

A drop shot is a ball played just over the net. You play it with underspin, which gives your shot less forward momentum and your opponent less time to cover the court to reach it. Drop shots are best played from your opponent's topspin shots rather than their sliced ones, and from a lower contact position rather than a high one. They are especially valuable against baseliners, who typically don't run forward as well as they do laterally.

Drop volleys are drop shots made from the net. They are devastating because your opponent has almost no time to react. Disguised drop shots are the most effective— they appear to be normal groundstrokes or volleys, but at the last possible moment, the racquet face opens and a deceptive drop shot is played.

1 During the forward swing, keep your hand high, and quickly change to a volley grip. Play a high-to-low shot for underspin, which slows the ball down after it has bounced.

2 Open the racquet face into contact and play a delicate shot just over the net. The follow-through is short, with the racquet face ending up completely open.

3 After a well-executed drop shot, move forward in preparation to make a winning shot from your opponent's weak reply.

approach shots

When your opponent hits a short ball, attack it! Using an approach shot is one effective way to play attacking tennis. It means playing a groundstroke and then moving forward, taking up an aggressive net position. Use an approach shot when your opponent's shot is short.

To keep your opponent guessing and on the defensive, you should include the approach into your repertoire of shots and use it at every opportunity. To use your approach shots effectively, hit them down the line when the ball is wide and crosscourt from near the center.

WATCH IT
see DVD chapter 7

a Lean on it
For an effective approach shot using a backhand slice, hit it hard and low over the net, making the ball skid through. To achieve this, lean into the ball while playing the shot.

b Quick start
For a quick start toward the net while making a forehand approach, keep moving forward while playing the shot.

c Finish the shot
When playing a backhand approach shot, be sure to finish it properly by completing your follow-through before opening up and running toward the net.

d Move in
When you make an approach shot and manage to force a weak reply, don't let the ball drop. Play your volley well above net height for power and better angles.

passing shots

When your opponent hits an approach shot, you will need to make a passing shot. These are groundstrokes that are placed past your opponent when they are at the net. They can be played either down the line or crosscourt. Hit them low over the net and with pace to give your opponent less time to react.

Before you attempt to play good passing shots, test your opponent's volleying skills. If their skills are weak, aim your passing shot well inside the lines. When your opponent has good volleying skills, make them stretch to reach the ball.

WATCH IT
see DVD chapter 7

Hit through

When you realize that your opponent is about to play an approach shot, you need to be aggressive and, when you can, play your passing shot with topspin.

Stay down

When playing your passing shots, stay down. This will help you to play the shot low over the net, and force your opponent to volley up. Staying low also helps you to react quickly to the next shot.

Tactics

When facing an opponent who constantly approaches the net, you should vary the direction of your passing shots so you don't become predictable. A net player will then have a difficult time anticipating the direction of your passing shot, losing valuable time and therefore making your future passing shots more effective. A dipping, crosscourt passing shot will make the net player stretch and, if they reach the ball, it will force them to play a great volley to win the point.

C

go further

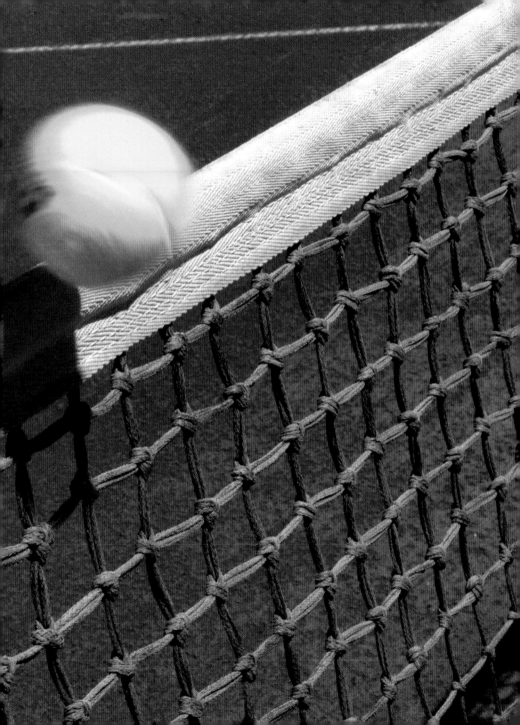

coming up...

Shaping up: 136–41

To be a tough opponent, you must play to your strengths and take advantage of your opponent's weaknesses. The right physical exercises will help your game, and make you a challenging opponent at your club and local tournaments.

Styles of play: 142–45

Learning to recognize and understand different playing styles, such as that of baseline players or net players, helps you to form a winning game plan. Playing against someone with a different style than your own can make a match more interesting

Tennis and travel: 148–51

Many tennis enthusiasts combine a dream vacation to a country they wish to visit with a tournament, and get to see the greats play live. The four grand slams are the biggest tournaments in tennis, and they always feature the best players in the world. Here's where to find out more.

pre-play warm-ups

Regular tennis players know how vital it is to warm up before starting play. A few simple stretches can help improve your performance and protect you from potential injury.

Stretching loosens your muscles, which enables better mobility. When fully warmed up, you should be ready to stretch out for those hard-to-reach shots without causing injury.

The following exercises will help to loosen you up; in each case, repeat on both sides of the body, go gently, and stop if you feel any pain.

Triceps
Bend one arm behind your head and touch your shoulder. With the other hand, pull your elbow to stretch the tricep.

Shoulder and upper back
Stretch one arm across your chest and use the opposite forearm to pull the arm toward you and intensify the stretch.

Quadriceps stretch
Hold the net for support. Raise one leg behind you and pull the foot toward you with your hand. Hold for 10 seconds.

Thigh stretch
Step forward with one leg. Bend the other, keeping the heel slightly off the ground. Lower yourself down and hold for 10 seconds.

a

b

c

d

building your tennis muscles

If you're serious about competitive play, you will need to spend more time strengthening your muscles to enhance your play and protect your body.

Competitive tennis puts a lot of stress on the body and can cause injury, which postpones your playing and often means long, frustrating recovery time.

Areas that are especially vulnerable to injury for all tennis players, and which need to be strengthened, are the knees, lower back, shoulders, elbows, and wrists. An overall body strengthening plan is best, with special emphasis on these points.

- Exercises such as sit-ups and push-ups are beneficial for core stability and general conditioning.

- A professional trainer can advise you on the weights to purchase for home use to strengthen the wrists and the important muscles for the elbows and shoulders.

- Don't stick with just one sport or exercise routine. Exercises such as jogging and skipping can help build your stamina.

being a competitor

When entering tournaments, you'll soon realize that nerves play a big part—the pressure of competition is more intense than friendly matches. Pressure can be used to push your game, but it takes a while to do this. Make sure you don't add to the pressure by following these simple rules.

- Decide to have fun and give your best in every point, regardless of the outcome.
- Arrive early and get physically and mentally prepared. Stretch and get warmed up by practicing with another player or hitting a ball against a wall.
- Make sure you have an extra racquet and a new can of balls.
- Don't forget to bring water, extra socks, sunblock, bandages, and a towel.
- Make sure that you have optimum energy—eat three hours before you play.

a Be prepared
Have all the necessary equipment ready. When you have less to worry about, you can think about the match.

b Concentrate
Stay focused when playing. Don't let your eyes wander outside the boundaries of the court. You need to avoid unnecessary distractions.

c Check your racquet
During play—especially a competitive match—your strings will take a beating. Check them occasionally and shift them back into position.

baseliner

A baseliner plays from the back of the court, preferring to trade groundstrokes rather than come up to the net. There are two types of baseliner: an aggressive baseliner and a counterpuncher.

An aggressive baseliner likes to dominate. They stand on or very near the baseline, take the ball early, and power their shots into the open court. Their goal is to wear down their opponents, both physically and mentally.

A counterpuncher uses their speed, fitness, and patience to maximum effect. They are fantastic at defending, and pass with pinpoint accuracy. They have learned to use the drop shot effectively, and play the lob to perfection at pivotal moments in the match.

• When playing an aggressive baseliner, move quickly. Reaching their best shots and placing them back into court makes them hit more shots, giving them an extra opportunity to miss.

• If you are an aggressive baseliner, your opponent will need to hit good shots constantly to stay in the point.

• To play against a counterpuncher, you must be patient, try to force a weak shot and then attack.

• If you are a counterpuncher, you can test your opponent's fitness with some long baseline rallies.

Winning points
Most two-handed backhand players are more comfortable being baseline players. Practice your volley and win some points the easy way.

Stay on the offensive
To be more effective as an aggressive baseliner, take every opportunity to move around your backhand to play a forehand. This tactic will keep your opponent constantly on the defensive.

WATCH IT
see DVD chapter 8

A net player stays at the front of the court as much as possible and plays as many shots as they can from the net. There are two types of net player—the all-around player and the net rusher—and both styles of play provide effective ways of winning a match.

net player

• Playing an all-arounder requires a calm attitude. Do what you are good at and look for their weak points, imposing your strengths on them.

• An all-around player can play every shot in tennis. When one style of play is not working, they can employ another style and therefore still have a good chance of winning the match.

• You need to stay mentally strong when playing a net rusher. Use the lob to keep them off guard.

• Being a net rusher forces your opponent to play better shots in order to win points.

a

WATCH IT
see DVD chapter 8

Service line
The serve-and-volleyer must get a quick start to the net. Their goal is to play the first volley from inside the service line.

Open court
Hit your approach shots with power and depth and then move toward the net, playing your first volley to the open court.

Play deep
Net play requires quick hands and superb athletic movement. When you are in trouble, remember to play the ball deep and to the backhand side.

Net result
Volley your opponent's high and wide shot down the line and their low shots crosscourt. You will then be well positioned for the next volley.

the major tournaments

The major tournaments in tennis are the four grand slams: The Australian Open, French Open, Wimbledon, and the US Open. Many tennis enthusiasts organize vacations to countries hosting grand slam tournaments. This way, they can enjoy a dream vacation to a country they wish to visit and at the same time get to see the greats play. The four grand slams are the biggest tournaments in tennis and they always feature the best players in the world, both men and women. Each one is held for two weeks at different times of the year.

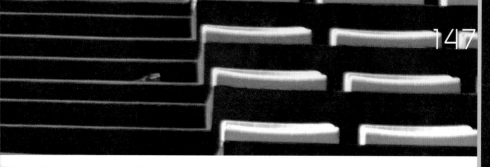

a The Australian Open

The first grand slam of the year is the Australian Open. It has a magnificent venue, Melbourne Park (formerly Flinders Park) in Melbourne. It takes place in early January, and players must be fit to combat the midsummer heat. It's played on Rebound Ace, a rubbery hard surface designed to be player-friendly. This surface favors play from the baseline and the net. Fans enjoy the friendly atmosphere of the Australian Open, and the contact they have with players on the outside courts.

b The French Open

The French Open is the second grand slam tournament of the year. It is held at Roland Garros, Paris, in late May or early June. The court surface is clay, which favors baseline play. Long rallies and hard-fought points can be seen in most matches. Net players rarely do well at the French Open. The clash of styles can bring an exciting mix of play, and this battle of wits often brings the crowd to its feet. It is usually clay court specialists who are extremely fit and patient that win at the French.

a

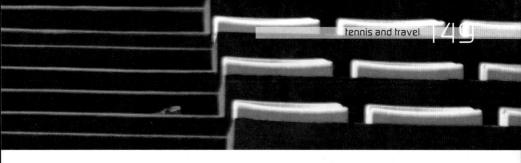

Wimbledon

The third and most prestigious of the grand slam tournaments is Wimbledon. Also known as "The Championships," they are held in London, England at the All England Lawn Tennis Club. This is the tournament that all professional players dream of winning, and it takes place during the last week of June and the first week of July. It's played on grass courts and heavily favors the serve and volleyer. Wimbledon was the inaugural grand slam tournament and the name is synonymous with tradition in tennis.

The US Open

The last grand slam tournament of the year is the US Open. It is held at Flushing Meadows, New York, from late August to early September. It is hot and humid and players must be extremely fit to make it through the two weeks. The tournament is played on hard courts and the speed of the surface allows aggressive baseliners and all-around players to excel. The Big Apple crowds are rowdy and support their favorite players with enthusiasm, which gives this tournament a special atmosphere.

great locations

Tennis resorts are situated in many beautiful and interesting locations around the world, and a tennis vacation presents a great opportunity to combine playing your favorite sport with visiting stunning destinations.

From basic court and racquet hire to intensive one-on-one tuition, there is a huge range of facilities and instruction available. You can find information on resort locations and the facilities available on the internet, in specialist brochures, and in tennis magazines. Whatever your level, at most resorts, you can choose to play any number of tennis hours in various combinations, and tuition ranges from short private lessons to group sessions of up to five hours. Group sessions can be fun and often focus on specific shots and tactics for playing both singles and doubles. Tennis "camps" offer a great way to work on your tennis game and physical conditioning with like-minded people.

Of course, tennis vacations can also incorporate sightseeing, adventure sports, shopping, cultural visits, and sun worshiping. Whether you travel in a group or by yourself, tennis offers you the chance to meet people from all over the world.

Tennis hotspots

The reach of tennis, as a truly global sport, means that great destinations for tennis-based vacations and travel are located all over the world.

- Blessed with year-round sun, luxurious resorts, and renowned tennis academies, Florida is viewed by most as the center of world tennis.

- Spain boasts some of the world's best tennis resorts, offering stunning locations, excellent facilities, and high standards of tuition.

- With a strong tennis tradition, excellent clubs, and its own Grand Slam tournament, Australia is a prime destination for a tennis-based vacation.

- Home of one of the world's most prolific tournament systems, France offers travelers lots of great tennis and lovely scenery.

- Dubai's emergence as a top vacation spot has seen the establishment of many fine tennis and leisure resorts as well as a tournament on the professional circuit.

tennis on the web

The internet is an easy way to access information about tennis. Everything from becoming a member of your national tennis association to buying equipment can be done on the web. Search for stores online or look in tennis magazines to find reputable sites.

If you want to play tennis at tournament level, you will need to join your national tennis association. Through their websites you will find all you need to become a member. They also have information on clubs and facilities and useful links to other sites.

USA
www.usta.com

UK
www.lta.org.uk

REPUBLIC OF IRELAND
www.tennisireland.ie

AUSTRALIA
www.tennisaustralia.com.au

SOUTH AFRICA
www.satennis.co.za

NEW ZEALAND
www.tennisnz.com/

CANADA
www.tenniscanada.com/

The International Tennis Federation is the world governing body of tennis. Their website gives the latest information on the professional circuit. You will find the tournament calendar, dates, results, statistics, rankings, player info, rules and regulations, and more.
www.itftennis.com

For information about grand slam tournaments, use their official websites. When a grand slam is in progress, you will get the latest updates on matches, pictures of the day, and player info.

THE AUSTRALIAN OPEN
www.australianopen.com

THE FRENCH OPEN
www.fft.fr/rolandgarros/

WIMBLEDON
www.wimbledon.com

THE US OPEN
www.usopen.org

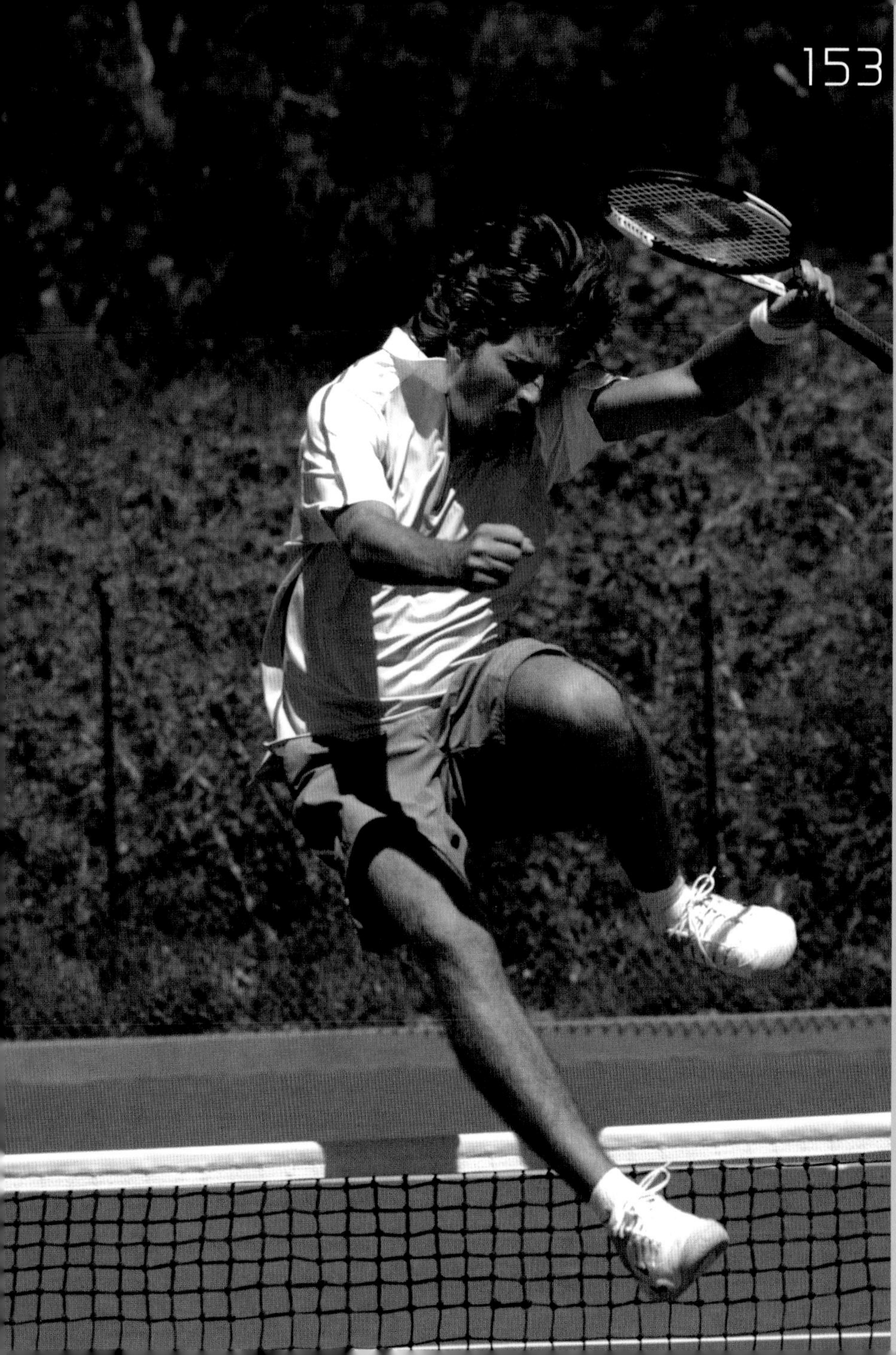

tennis talk

Advantage server/receiver: The advantage point is the one played after deuce. When the server wins the deuce point, it is called advantage "in." When the receiver wins the deuce point, it is called advantage "out."

All-around player: A player who has a good command of all the shots in tennis and can adopt any style of play.

Angled shot: Any shot played across the net in an attempt to take the opponent out of court.

Approach shot: A shot played just before going to the net.

Backswing: When the racquet moves back and away from the oncoming ball.

Baseliner: Players who prefer to compete from the baseline.

Bevel: The flat sides of the racquet handle.

Breaking serve: Winning the game when receiving serve.

Counterpuncher: A player who reacts to and counters the forcing play of an opponent.

Clay court: A court surface made from either red or green clay.

Crosscourt: When the ball goes from one side of one end of the court to the diagonal side of the other end.

Crossover step: When one leg comes up to and across the other.

Deuce: When the point score in a game stands at 40–40. A player needs two consecutive points from deuce to win the game.

Dink shot: A shot played just over the net, with the intention of landing the ball at the opponent's feet.

Doubles alley: The area of the court outside the singles lines to the outer sidelines. These are used for doubles play.

Double fault: The loss of a point by making consecutive missed serves.

Doubles: A match played between two teams of two players each.

Down the line: A shot played from either side of the court hitting the ball straight instead of crosscourt.

Drop shot: A ball played just over the net with little forward momentum.

End: Refers to the playing area on either side of the net.

Fault: A serve that lands outside the service box.

Flat feet: Refers to movement made without the use of the calf muscles.

Follow-through: The path of the racquet after making contact with the ball.

Footwork: The series of steps used to reach the ball, or to position yourself for your next shot.

Forced error: A missed shot caused by the good play of an opponent.

Game: A scoring unit counted toward a set.

Groundstroke: A type of shot usually made from around the baseline and after the ball has bounced.

Gut string: A high-performance racquet string made from natural fibers.

Half-volley: A shot played just after the ball has bounced (see Volley).

Hard court: A court surface made from a hard material such as cement.

Holding serve: Winning the game as the server.

Let: Something that disrupts play and requires a replay of the point. Let also refers to the serve being played again after the ball hits the net tape and falls inside the service box.

Lob: A ball played high over the net.

Love: Used in place of zero when scoring.

Match: A competitive format with the winner decided using the scoring system of tennis.

Mid-size: A racquet with a head size of between 85 sq. in (550 sq. cm) and 95 sq. in (610 sq. cm).

Net chord: A shot that hits the net and then lands inside the opponent's court.

Overgrip: A thin disposable grip placed over the permanent grip of the handle.

Over-size: A racquet with a head size of between 95 sq. in (610 sq. cm) and 110 sq. in (710 sq. cm).

Point: A scoring unit counted toward a game.

Racquet face: The strung hitting surface of a racquet where contact with the ball is made.

Racquet throat: The area between the racquet head and the handle.

Ready position: The position a player takes before the ball approaches.

Recovery steps: The steps needed to get into position after retrieving and hitting an opponent's shot.

Restring: When the set of strings on a racquet is taken out and replaced with a new set.

Sanctioned tournament: A tournament that is registered by the tennis association of the country in which it takes place.

Serve and volleyer: A player who often advances to the net after making a serve.

Set: A scoring unit counted toward a match.

Shot selection: The type of shot a player chooses to use in any given circumstance.

Side: The playing area on either side of the center mark is referred to as a side. The "deuce" court, where every game is started, is on the right-hand side when facing the net. The "ad" court is the left side of the court when facing the net.

Sidespin: When the ball spins horizontally.

Side-step: Steps you need to make when moving sideways.

Singles sticks: Sticks that are used to prop up the net at the side of the court. They are only used for singles play.

Singles: A match played between two people.

Sitter: A high ball close to the net that gives an easy opportunity to play a winner.

Smart play: A series of shots used to move your opponent out of play.

Smash: An aggressive and powerful shot played above head height.

Spin: Imparting spin is making the ball rotate after a shot is played.

Split-step: Separating the feet while the opponent is hitting the ball.

String tension: The tightness to which the strings were pulled during stringing.

Sweet spot: The area of the hitting surface that gives maximum response when contacting the ball.

Tie-breaker: A scoring system used to decide a set when the game score reaches 6 all.

Topspin: When the ball spins forward after contact is made.

Underspin: When the ball spins backward after contact is made.

Unforced error: A missed shot due to poor concentration rather than the opponent's forcing play.

Vibration dampener: A small rubber device that is placed between the strings, and below the bottom string, which greatly decreases racquet vibration.

Volley: Refers to the types of shots that are usually played up at the net before the ball has bounced.

Weight transfer: Shifting body weight from one leg to another.

Winner: Any shot played that was not reached by the opponent before the second bounce.

Work the point: Using a series of shots to move an opponent out of position.

index

index

and finally...

Thanks from the author

A special thanks to Stephanie Farrow for her trust and support throughout this project.

My heartfelt thanks to Nicky Munro and Jenisa Patel, the lovely and brilliant editor and designer at DK, with whom I've worked so closely throughout this project and to whom I'm deeply grateful.

An appreciative thanks to José and Carol at Club del Sol for hosting the shoot and for their kind hospitality.

Thanks to the photographer, Gerard Brown and designer Nigel Wright for their diligent pursuit of the perfect picture.

Cheers to Gez at Chrome productions for putting together a terrific DVD.

A big thanks to the models; Marielle Wallin, Ellie Beaton, and Joe Beaton for lending their amazing talents to this project and for their tireless effort and enthusiasm throughout the shoot.

Thanks from Dorling Kindersley

DK would like to thank May Corfield and Letty Luff for editorial assistance, and Margaret McCormack for indexing.
Also many thanks to Club del Sol for the use of their great tennis courts, and to Wilson for providing the tennis racquets.

Club del Sol
C/D José de Orbaneja s/n
Urb. Sitio de Calahonda
29647 Mijas-Costa (Malaga)
Tel: +34 952 93 95 95
Web site: www.tenniscostadelsol.com

Thanks for the pictures

17b, 32 The Image Bank, photograph by Moritz Steiger; 146b Getty, photograph by Nick Laham; 147b Getty, photograph by Clive Mason; 148b Getty, photograph by Phil Cole; 149b Getty photograph by Ezra Shaw; 150 Stone, photograph by Hiroshi Nomura; 151 The Image Bank, photograph by John Kelly.